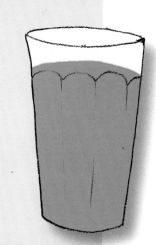

Healthy Eating

All kinds of
Drinks

Susan Martineau
and Hel James

W

FRANKLIN WATTS
LONDON•SYDNEY

 An Appleseed Editions book

First published in 2006 by Franklin Watts

Paperback edition 2008

Franklin Watts
338 Euston Road, London NW1 3BH

Franklin Watts Australia
Level 17/207 Kent Street, Sydney NSW 2000

Created by Appleseed Editions Ltd,
Well House, Friars Hill, Guestling, East Sussex TN35 4ET

Designed and illustrated by Helen James
Edited by Jinny Johnson

ISBN 978 0 7496 8172 2

Dewey Classification: 641.2

A CIP catalogue for this book is available from the British Library

Photographs: 10 Owen Franken/Corbis; 13 David Aubrey/Corbis; 16 Franz-Marc Frei/Corbis;
18 So Hing-Keung/Corbis; 20-21 Kelly-Mooney Photography/Corbis; 22 Owen Franken/Corbis;
24 Neil Rabinowitz/Corbis; 27 Owen Franken/Corbis; 28 Ron Sanford/Corbis.
Front cover: PhotoCuisine/Corbis

Printed in China

Franklin Watts is a division
of Hachette Children's Books

Contents

Food for health   4

A balanced plateful!   6

We need water   8

A drink from the tap   10

Water from a bottle   12

Fruit in a glass   14

Milk, smoothies and shakes   16

Fizzy drinks   18

Squashes   20

A cup of coffee   22

What about tea?   24

Chocolate drinks   26

A word about alcohol   28

Words to remember   30

Index and websites   32

Food for health

Our bodies are like amazing machines.
Just like machines, we need the right
sort of fuel to give us energy and
to keep us working properly.

If we don't eat the kind of food we need to keep us healthy we may become ill or feel tired and grumpy. Our bodies don't really like it if we eat too much of one sort of food, like cakes or chips.

We need a balanced diet. That means eating different sorts of good food in the right amounts.

You'll be surprised at how much there is to know about where our food comes from and why some kinds of food are better for us than others. Finding out about food is great fun and very tasty!

I'm really thirsty.

We need to make sure we have enough to drink each day. Drinks are fuel for our bodies too.

Let's go and have a drink of water.

A balanced plateful!

The good things or nutrients our bodies need come from different kinds of food. Let's have a look at what your plate should have on it. It all looks delicious!

Water
We need to drink at least 6 glasses of water every day.

Fruit and vegetables

Rice, bread and pasta

Rice, bread and pasta

These foods contain carbohydrates and they give us energy. About a third of our food should come from this group.

Fruit and vegetables

These are full of great vitamins and minerals and fibre and they help keep you healthy. About a third of our food should come from this group.

Meat, fish and eggs

Protein from these helps your body grow and repair itself. They are body-building foods and we need to eat them every day.

Milk, yogurt and cheese

These dairy foods give us protein and also calcium to make strong bones and teeth.

Sugar and fats

We only need small amounts of these. Too much can be bad for our teeth and make us fat.

Milk, yogurt and cheese

Sugar and fats

Meat, fish and eggs

We need water

Our bodies have lots of water in them. Even the parts of you that look solid contain water. We can keep going for several weeks without food, but we cannot last more than a few days without water.

When we pee or sweat we lose water from our bodies. We even lose water when we are breathing! We need to replace this water so that our bodies feel all right. Without enough water our bodies dehydrate and cannot work properly.

I get thirsty when I'm running around.

If you feel thirsty you are already dehydrating. Have a drink!

DRINKS LIST
Breakfast

Have a big glass of milk with your breakfast.

We get some water from the food we eat, but we still need to make sure we drink lots every day. Some drinks are better for us than others and the very best one of all is WATER.

DRINKS LIST
Lunch

A fresh fruit juice is delicious with your sandwich.

DRINKS LIST
Dinner

A drink of water is refreshing at suppertime.

Juicy fruit like watermelon, grapes and oranges give our bodies water too.

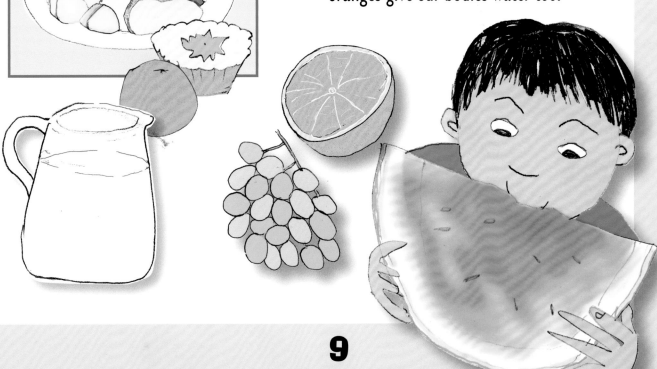

A drink from the tap

Have you ever thought about the journey water has to make before you can turn on the tap and have a drink?

All our water comes from rain or snow. Rain, or water from melted snow, runs into streams and rivers. It can be collected in a reservoir. This is a lake that is built specially to store water for us.

The water is cleaned and made safe for us to drink. Then it goes along pipes to a storage tank. After that, more pipes bring it into your house all ready for you to use.

Rain and snow

Reservoir

Pipes

Water treatment

Storage tank

Pipes

You could keep a chart to see who drinks the most water in your family.

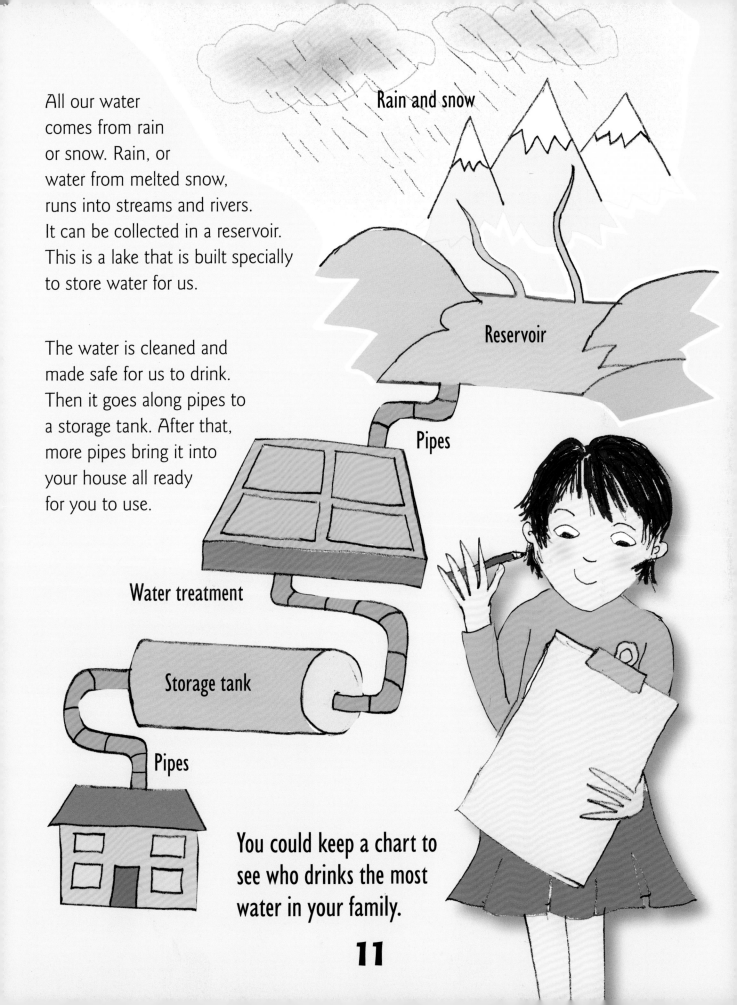

11

Water from a bottle

You can buy water in bottles. It is called mineral water or spring water. It comes from under the ground and is collected and bottled. It is a handy drink when you are out and about and not near a tap!

Time for a water break!

Some bottled water is called 'still', which means it does not have any fizz in it. 'Sparkling' water is fizzy and bubbly.

Some bottled waters have flavourings added, like lemon, lime or raspberry. But these also have sugar added to them so they are not good for your teeth.

Some people like to use water filter jugs. These give the water an extra clean and make it taste even nicer.

Pop a slice of lemon or lime in a glass of water for an extra refreshing taste.

Fruit in a glass

You can get all sorts of delicious juices to drink. Juices can be made from one fruit or a mixture of fruit. They can also be made using vegetables like carrots and celery. Juices have lots of good vitamins in them to keep you healthy.

Try to choose fruit juices labelled 'pure fruit juice' and not 'fruit drink'. The ones with the word 'drink' on the label do not contain much fruit and have extra sugar added.

All fruit juices have some sugar in them. It is best to have them with a meal so your teeth are not having a bath in sugar!

Choose pure juices.

Juice test

Make your own juice mixture and see if your friends can guess which fruit you have used. Use pure juices from cartons or make your own juice from peeled and seeded fruit and vegetables.

Carrot

Orange

Pineapple

Cranberry

Mango and passion fruit

Apple

Tomato

Milk, smoothies and shakes

Milk is a great drink. Most of the milk people drink comes from cows. Milk gives your body lots of great vitamins, body-building protein and calcium for strong bones and teeth.

Milk is a food as well as a drink. It has lots of good nutrients.

Smoothies and milkshakes are made out of fruit mixed with yogurt or milk. Yogurt is made from milk so it has the same good nutrients. The fruit adds extra vitamins.

The smoothies and shakes you can buy in the shops often have sugar added to them. If you whiz up your own with lovely, juicy, ripe fruit you will find that you do not need all that extra sugar.

Blueberries

Blackcurrants

Passion fruit

Bananas

Strawberries

Pineapple

I like my milk plain.

I like to add banana and strawberries to my milk.

If you are not very keen on plain milk or yogurt, milkshakes and smoothies are a good way of getting dairy goodness.

Fizzy drinks

Fizzy drinks, like colas and lemonades, contain loads of sugar. All fizzy drinks also have something called acid in them that attacks your teeth. So even drinks with 'diet' or 'low sugar' on the labels are not great for your teeth.

If you could put your teeth in a glass of cola you would see the harm it does. You could try it with any baby teeth you wobble out.

I'm so full of fizziness I don't want my supper!

'Diet' or 'low sugar' drinks have sweeteners in them instead of lots of sugar. But having too many sweeteners may not be very good for us either.

Fizzy drinks do not have many nutrients and they make you feel full up without giving your body any goodness. If you are full of fizz you might not feel like eating the balanced platefuls of healthy food that your body needs.

Sports or energy drinks are meant for people who are doing lots of sports. These drinks contain lots of sugar and caffeine. Unless you have just run a marathon, you do not really need them!

Squashes

Squashes are a juice drink that you make by adding water to a cordial. A cordial is a thick and sticky mixture made from fruit juice and sugar.

Flavourings and colourings are often added to cordials to give them extra taste and colour. These flavourings and colourings are tested to check they are safe for us to drink, but some people think they are not very good for us.

Apple and blackcurrant

Check labels to find cordials that have not been made with lots of extra flavours and colours added.

Lime

Cranberry and raspberry

Lemon and lime

Orange

There are all sorts of cordials. You can buy them in bottles to mix with water yourself or you can get them ready mixed.

Remember to add lots of water.

Lemon

21

A cup of coffee

Coffee is made from beans that grow on a coffee tree. The beans grow inside coffee berries and they are the seeds of the trees. There are two beans inside each berry.

This girl has just picked some coffee berries. Inside are coffee beans.

When they are a nice red colour the berries are ready to be picked. The beans are then taken out and roasted. Coffee is made by grinding up the beans into powder and then pouring boiling water on it.

Some people like coffee with milk. Others like it black – without milk.

This mug of coffee is for Dad.

Coffee has something called caffeine in it. Cola drinks often contain caffeine too. Caffeine makes you pee more and this means your body loses more water than it needs to. Too much caffeine can also make you feel jumpy and give you headaches.

What about tea?

Tea is made out of the dried leaves of a bush. Tea bushes were first grown in China but they are now grown in lots of other countries too.

Black tea

Green tea

The tea leaves are picked by hand. Only the buds and top two leaves of the bush are picked. The leaves are partly dried, cut or crushed and left until they turn a red colour. Then they are dried some more.

Like coffee, tea is not the best drink for children because it also contains caffeine. If you want to have a cup of tea you could try teas made out of herbs and fruit instead.

You can buy tea in boxes or bags. To make a cup of tea you need to pour boiling water over the leaves or the teabag.

I'm going to try some rosehip tea today.

25

Chocolate drinks

Chocolate drinks are made using cocoa powder. This is made out of the seeds of the cacao tree. The seeds, or beans, of the trees grow inside large pods. The trees grow in South America, West Africa and Indonesia.

Other ingredients, like milk powder and sugar, are added to the powdered cocoa. The mixture is then stirred into hot milk or water to make a tasty, warming drink.

Cocoa contains some caffeine so it is best not to drink too much of it. But having a mug of hot chocolate every now and then can be a great way to drink milk if you do not like milk on its own. Milk gives you vitamins and loads of calcium for strong bones and teeth.

You can buy lots of different chocolate drinks.

Cacao beans were used as money by the Aztecs who lived in Mexico hundreds of years ago.

A word about alcohol

There are lots of different drinks that contain alcohol. Wine, cider and beer are all alcoholic drinks.

Wine is made from grapes. Cider is made from apples. Beer is made from a grain called barley. Yeast is used to turn the sugar in the fruit and grain into alcohol.

Red wine　White wine

Cider

Vodka

Whisky

Gin

Brandy

Beer

When you drink alcohol it gets into your blood. It slows your brain down and makes it hard for you to control your movements and feel like yourself. Too much alcohol can hurt your liver, heart, brain and stomach.

In the United Kingdom it is against the law to buy alcohol before you are 18 years old.

Alcohol is bad for growing bodies. If children drink alcohol it does more harm to them because their bodies are smaller than grown-up ones.

Alcopops

Alcopops are drinks that look like flavoured lemonades and colas but they have alcohol in them. They are not good for children.

29

Words to remember

acid   Acids are sour-tasting liquids. Lemon juice and vinegar are acids. Acids can damage your teeth.

caffeine   Caffeine is found in coffee, tea, chocolate and colas. It makes you pee more and can upset your stomach. It can also stop you being able to sleep.

calcium   A mineral that helps build healthy bones and teeth. Dairy foods, like milk, yogurt and cheese, have calcium in them.

carbohydrates   Starches and sugars in food that give us energy. Carbohydrate foods are rice, pasta, bread and potatoes.

colourings   Colourings are put into lots of drinks like squashes and fizzy drinks. Some people think that some of these are not very good for us and that they can make children a bit jumpy.

dairy   Dairy foods are made from milk. They include yogurt, cheese, cream and butter.

dehydrate   We dehydrate when our bodies do not get enough water. It can make us feel dizzy and tired. Being thirsty is a sign that you are already dehydrating.

fibre   Fibre is found in plant foods like fruit and vegetables. It helps our insides to work properly.

flavourings   These are added to foods to change the way they taste or to make the taste stronger. Fruit drinks, squashes and fizzy drinks often contain flavourings.

ingredients   Different foods that are mixed together to make something we can eat or drink.

minerals   Nutrients in food that help our bodies work properly. Calcium is a mineral.

nutrients   Parts of food that your body needs for energy, to grow healthily and to repair itself.

protein   Body-building food that makes our bodies grow well and stay healthy.

reservoir   A lake specially built to store water.

storage tank   A very large container where clean water can be kept ready for people to use.

sweeteners   These are chemicals that are added to drinks and foods to make them taste sweet. They have long names like aspartame and acesulfame-K. Have a look at the lists of ingredients on labels to see if they are included. Some people think that these sweeteners may not be very good for our bodies.

vitamins   Nutrients in food that help our bodies work properly.

yeast   Yeast is added to fruit or grain to make the sugar in them turn into alcohol.

Index

alcohol 28-29

balanced diet 4, 6-7
bottled water 12-13

caffeine 19, 23. 25-26, 30
chocolate drinks 26-27
cocoa 26-27
coffee 22-23
cola 19, 23
cordials 20-21

fizzy drinks 18-19
fruit juice 14-15, 20

milk and milkshakes 16-17

smoothies 17
sparkling water 13
sports drinks 19
squashes 20-21
still water 13

tea 24-25

water 6, 8-9, 10-11
water filter 13

yogurt 17

WEBSITES

General food information for all ages
www.bbc.co.uk/health/healthy_living/nutrition

Food Standards Agency – healthy eating, food labelling
www.eatwell.gov.uk

Quizzes and games on food
www.coolfoodplanet.org

Information and games on healthy eating
www.lifebytes.gov.uk/eating/eat_menu.html

Worksheets and activities
www.foodforum.org.uk

Practical advice on healthy eating
www.fitness.org.uk